DO YOU KNOW

Rats?

Written by
Alain M. Bergeron
Michel Quintin
Sampar

Illustrations by
Sampar

Translated by
Solange Messier

Fitzhenry & Whiteside

Published in Canada by Fitzhenry & Whiteside, 195 Allstate Parkway, Markham, Ontario L3R 4T8
Published in the United States by Fitzhenry & Whiteside, 311 Washington Street, Brighton, Massachusetts 02135

www.fitzhenry.ca godwit@fitzhenry.ca
10 9 8 7 6 5 4 3 2 1

Library and Archives Canada Cataloguing in Publication
Do You Know Rats?
ISBN 978-1-55455-319-8 (pbk.)
Data available on file

Publisher Cataloging-in-Publication Data (U.S.)
Bergeron, Alain M.
Do you know rats?/ Alain M. Bergeron ; Michel Quintin ; illustrations by Sampar ; translated by Solange Messier.
Originally published in French as: Savais-tu? les rats; Waterloo, Quebec: Éditions Michel Quintin, 2008.
[64] p. : col. ill. ; cm.
Summary: Fascinating and informative facts about rats presented in graphic novel format.
ISBN: 978-1-55455-319-8 (pbk.)
1. Rats – Juvenile literature. I. Quintin, Michel. II. Sampar. III. Messier, Solange. IV. Title.
599.35/2 dc23   QL737.R666B374 2013

Fitzhenry & Whiteside acknowledges with thanks the Canada Council for the Arts, and the Ontario Arts Council for their support of our publishing program. We acknowledge the financial support of the Government of Canada through the Canada Book Fund (CBF) for our publishing activities.

Canada Council
for the Arts

Conseil des Arts
du Canada

ONTARIO ARTS COUNCIL
CONSEIL DES ARTS DE L'ONTARIO

50 YEARS OF ONTARIO GOVERNMENT SUPPORT OF THE ARTS
50 ANS DE SOUTIEN DU GOUVERNEMENT DE L'ONTARIO AUX ARTS

Text design by Daniel Choi
Cover image by Sampar
Printed in Canada by Friesens Corporation

MIX
Paper from
responsible sources
FSC
www.fsc.org
FSC® C016245

Rats are gnawing mammals called **rodents**. They can be found all over the world.

There are many **species** of rats. However, only brown rats and black rats live near humans. These two species live in cities, villages, farms and harbours.

The brown rat is the most widespread of all species. It has many names, such as common rat, street rat, sewer rat, and Norway rat.

9

Rats can be found in houses, barns, silos, warehouses, dumps, sewers and boats.

It's estimated that there are four rats for every person in the city. Even more rats reside in the country.

Rats dig complicated and intricate **burrows**. They establish their nests deep within these burrows.

Rats dig their burrows under buildings, in piles of garbage at dumps, and in fields.

In addition to being good diggers, rats are also great climbers and excellent swimmers.

19

Rats eat fruits, vegetables, grains, animals, **carrion** and garbage. In fact, they eat almost anything.

Rats also **prey** on small farm animals, such as chickens, ducks, and piglets.

Rats are intelligent creatures. Thanks to their fine sense of smell, they learn quickly to avoid poisoned bait.

Because rats reproduce in abundance and are quick to adapt, humans haven't been able to exterminate them.

Female rats can begin having babies when they are as young as 14 weeks old.

When a female rat is **in heat**, she can mate with more than six different males.

Although rats have an average of 6 litters of babies per year, they can have as many as 12.

Rats have an average of 8 babies per litter but can have as many as 22. The babies are born hairless and blind.

In ideal conditions, a rat couple and its offspring could, in 3 years, produce up to 20 million descendants.

Rats live in **hierarchies** where the largest males dominate the group.

Members of the same clan recognize one another through their scents.

Rats are aggressive and combative. They do not tolerate members of
other rat colonies entering their territory.

Sometimes, the winner of a rat fight will cover his rival in urine as a sign of victory.

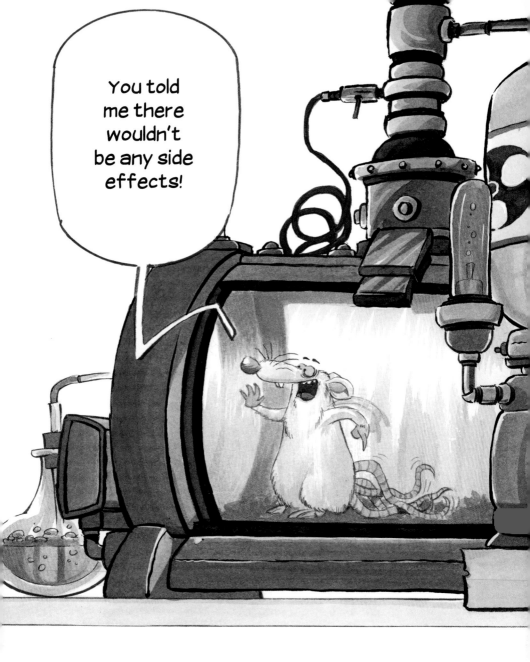

The white rat used in lab experiments is actually a type of albino brown rat.

Rats have plenty of **predators**. Humans, cats, dogs, foxes, coyotes, birds, and many other animals prey on them.

In the wild, a rat's life expectancy is approximately three years.

The rat is considered the most destructive **mammal** on earth.

Each year, rats cause enormous losses to humans by eating and contaminating food. They also cause a lot of destruction by gnawing on electric wires, building structures, etc.

One hundred rats in a warehouse could eat one tonne of grains in a year.

In a single day, the same 100 rats could soil a tonne of grains with over 5,000 droppings and a litre of urine.

Rats transmit several fatal diseases to humans, like the **plague**. They are likely responsible for more human deaths than all wars and revolutions combined.

Glossary

Burrow   a tunnel or hole dug in the ground

Carrion   dead or decaying animal flesh

Hierarchy   a group structure where group members are ranked by status or ability

In heat   ready to mate and reproduce

Mammal   a warm-blooded, back-boned animal

Plague   a dangerous and contagious bacterial disease, which is often spread by rats

Predator   a hunter that kills prey for food

Prey   an organism hunted and killed by another for food

Rodent   gnawing mammals, which include mice, rats, and hamsters

Species   a classification for a group of organisms with common characteristics

Index

Do You Know there are other titles?

Porcupines

Crows

Crocodiles

Leeches

Chameleons

Toads

Spiders